Praise

Dead Birds &

◆

"*John Bowie's collection of poetry is a nod to the disenchanted travellers who speak the truth. The writer is a wordsmith of the highest degree, shaping poetry that conveys days struck by melancholy and unmistakable pain. Dead Birds & Sinking Ships is not a love story, or one connected to innocence, it is an assessment of the human condition, drunken dazes, hardship, and hopelessness. Bowie is a true craftsman, creating worlds and words that will make the reader reflect on their own time on earth. This forward-thinking and intelligent compendium will provoke response as it delivers poetry on a whole new level, one that many poets cannot grasp. And Bowie is as natural a poet as he is a novelist, sprinkling his magic with dark lines and original content. It is his time to truly shine and conquer.*"

— **Mark McConville**, Music Journalist

"*Bowie's poetry is brutal and lyrical, beautifully textured, almost palpable. In Dead Birds & Sinking Ships, he depicts the contradictory world in which he grew up. A world of nature against urbanisation, reason against madness, a world of fights, real and imaginary, a world in which love, war, loneliness and trauma cohabit, that he exposes it in all its fascinating cruelty. A wonderful collection.*"

— **B F Jones**, author of, *The Fabric of Tombstones*

"*In the darker spectrum of fiction, John Bowie has become synonymous with the sordid bleakness of his settings and characters, while punctuating an inherent sentimental and Gothic beauty. In his first poetry collection, he elevates barstool frowns into birds soaring wayward above all this. A true man-versus-the-world who's got the guts to seek universal strength in the weaknesses of the human condition, yet not without an occasional stark judgment for those who have gone beyond the brinks of redemption. An Earthshackled-romantic body of work.*"

— **Gabriel Hart,** author of, *Virgins In Reverse* and *The Intrusion*; singer/songwriter of Jail Weddings

Dead Birds & Sinking Ships

(happy little tales of melancholy madness)

by

John Bowie

Close To The Bone Publishing

Contents

◆

About the Author

◆

John writes poetry, short stories and novels. His writing is a semi-autobiographical mix of dirty realism, crime fiction and noir.

His work has appeared online and in print for the likes of *Close To The Bone, Red Dog Press, Bristol Noir, Storgy Magazine, Litro Magazine, Punk Noir Magazine, Necro Magazine* and *Deadman's Tome.*

John grew up on the coast in rural Northumberland, a region steeped with a history of battles, Vikings, wars and struggles. These tales and myths fascinated him as a child, and then as an adult. In the mid to late nineties, he studied in Salford enjoying the bands, music, clubs and general urban industrialism of Greater Manchester, including the club scene and the infamous Hacienda. He was also there when the IRA bomb went off in 1996.

John now lives in Bristol with his wife and daughters, where he has been since the late nineties. He is a professional designer, artist and writer as well as a proud husband, father, brother and son.

He is the founder, curator and editor-in-chief of Bristol Noir.

His pulp-noir novel *Weston-super-Nightmare (Hellbent Riff Raff Thriller #1)* is out now with Close To The Bone.

Untethered and *Transference*, from John's Black Viking Thriller series, are out now with Red Dog Press.

For Chintzy, Sherry & Fred.

The most beautiful creatures have the sharpest teeth and claws, and still, we keep them close.

Foreword

◆

For those who might be new to the Indie noir scene, John Bowie is the editor of Bristol Noir and a brilliant novelist and poet.

I have been a massive fan of John Bowie ever since reading *Untethered*. He is an amazing writer, which is something I can say confidently as I'm about to finish his second book, *Transference*, and dive into his third novel, *Weston Super Nightmare*, and having been entrusted with writing the foreword of his poetry collection, *Dead Birds & Sinking Ships*, my admiration for the man has never ceased to grow.

In this first poetry collection, Bowie swaps his trademark wry humour for a deeply lyrical tone, inviting us to visit his soul, his memories, and to see the world through his eyes as a boy, a teenager, a man.

nature rattles outside
aching to share
to revel
to get in and at me.
to touch those dreams and memories
that shake inside:
futures;
fictions made free…

Bowie wraps ugly truths in stunning words, treating us to dirty realism at its best. He lays bare his painful memories of growing up and discovering the many cruelties of this world, this incremental loss of innocence from the moment he is exposed to the torture of a frog, through to the sex noises of a deceitful parent, the violence and trauma of war, the deceptions of love and the desperation drowned in pint glasses, temporarily making the world a better place only to come back the next day.

flick,
a spark,
then hopping flames.

stopping dead in the road.
flattened, as a car put it out
with a merciful tyre
that didn't stop.

he's not around anymore.
enlisted the next year,
earliest he could,
looking to quench a thirst.

He offers us broken fragments of a lifetime full of conflicts, a constant battle against pain, trauma, loneliness and addiction in a world in which nature fights urbanisation, birds die and ships sink, a world shown under the rusty, blood-coloured light of brutal and beautiful honesty.

she wouldn't let me in
I was kicked out for the day, maybe longer
whimpering like a dying limp
discarded
dog

she closed up, shut the door

the scar's still there
and now I'm old enough
that when I hurt,
like I do today,
more than I ever did then
I don't think
to go back
and it's when I should
and need it
most

not going back
to what was never there, to what I needed,
need now
I just bleed it out
Alone

A world where being kicked out of your house or the bar is much more of a guarantee than being allowed in. A world shown from the point of view of an outsider, struggling to fit in, to stay afloat, either too close or too far, too human, a body sinking in too many fluids, with blood, tears and liquor pouring throughout, clashing with the toughness, the hardness of the city, the army, the people, the past.

there's a window in my head,
left open by hurt
it's where the rain gets in
the curtains were never closed
thick,
still,
they blot out the light
letting in dark.

And this past, though littered with the bodies of innocent creatures, this fast-sinking youth, is referred to as *happy little tales of melancholy madness*, an interesting subtitle, a mini poem on its own. That summarises the collection and Bowie's world, out of which he extracts, tale-like memories, full of the raw sadness, happiness and insanity that make life worth living in the prospect of death.

when I thought,
I had nothing,
but had it
all
that I was trapped and lonely,
but was free
and going nowhere,

And this death, recurrent throughout the collection, and constantly looming, a sinking ship close to being boarded many times. However, he embarks onto a different boat, a small life vessel that makes fleeting yet recurrent appearances throughout the collection and that carries hope, love, music.

they weren't done with living yet.
bleeding ears, and blue rinses
didn't matter now.
they wanted to get to the solo

Music is a major element in Bowie's writing, there's a soundtrack to everything he writes, the hum of cities mixed with clubs and bars' background music, the celebration of decades of indie rock. And with the added lyricism of the poetry, the noir feel comes to life to the rhythm of broken hearts beating raw and alive, despite the dead birds, the deceptions, the suffering and the sinking ships.

B. F. Jones
April 2021

Dead Birds & Sinking Ships

(happy little tales of melancholy madness)

box made shallow from a body so deep (black butterflies)

the cold rests on his head, a slab his pillow.
looking to a hand, for lost comfort in images of faces
that come and go.
new and old friends pass by, as he reflects ashamed pains.
he pretends, hopes, he could be a little better — another day,
maybe tomorrow.

stardust and innocence spill from
happy, smiling children
skipping past.
their naive hopes burn
like napalm
over his cracked leathery skin.
he blows them away,
in a dead breath, made stagnant
on gasps of rerolled discarded fag ends.

they don't see
he's just another broken fixture
another cracked paving to ignore.
invisible.
and seeing them, makes him wish to stay
like that.
a dissolving fixture,
not influence or last over them.

he doesn't get the weather anymore. every day brings frost.
he knows what's coming.
the darkest season.

black butterflies visit, carrying thoughts of reason.
he waves at them — go away,
he has to.
to dwell now would be to give up altogether.
blacker visitors arrive
again. again.
he punches at them.
then himself.
hoping, for a chance, to start-over,
again,
someday.
to breathe life, again.

coins spill on and off,
in and out of a paper cup.
too little, too late,
from too few.
the community that cares, a little.
from a city that has failed altogether.
a mere dirty plaster on an amputated leg.

covered in stained broadsheets, tabloids.
words claiming importance, now meaningless.
unread sheets, now failed blankets.
their true lasting statement
made by his trembling body.
that feels the chills, regardless.

another Winter on the horizon.
with it comes the blackest of all butterflies
and he knows, he'll welcome them,
this time
no energy
to chase them away.

know your enemy

hello, old friend
long time, no see,
you've been around, the world
back now
I do see, I am listening
you've not settled down,
well done
you can see there was no point in that,
see it, yes
in me

I'll stroke your ego
confirm your life's decisions:
never making roots,
never working too hard
never feeling a woman's touch that wasn't paid for,
all taken not given

hello old friend
here's another with me tonight
you've not met them before

'cunts,' you say
— the both of us.
goodbye old friend
we did our best.

those roots you've never made
trail behind you,
drying out like seaweed in sun
rotting away in heavy lingering rains.

I hope you find shelter,
it won't be mine.

pull the trigger

where is he now?
just pull the trigger, will you,
so I don't have to.

he'd jumped out,
an arm around my neck,
a barrel to my temple.

his feigned aggression faded to fear
he could see I welcomed it.
he soon wished he hadn't pulled the joke
and, I wished he wasn't carrying blanks.

scorched sands, hopping frog

hey, come here.
why?
I want to show you something, the voice said from the gap.
I'm scared.
don't be a pussy.
come here...come under the roller shutters.
here in the garage, there's something real sweet. something I want to
show you...
now.
move — pussy.

I shook, petrified, as the shutters went up.
enough to let me, a 6 years small, under.
I went. steel gates shut down behind.
the doors clattered and shook. shut me in,
to a blackness. the garage. with him.

waning lights flickered,
a torch. a Zippo.
a hand grabbed,
pointed me at the workbench.
that's where evil happened.

look, I told you.
so sweet, isn't it.
LOOK.
I saw.
legs twitched in the vice.
a hiss and rasp came from a tiny helpless body.
check it out, he said.
taking a tin of lighter fluid he squeezed the nozzle
into a mouth forced painfully open,
and the tiny creature's body
squirmed.

it must have felt like acid.

before it could hope for release,
and poison took hold,
he undid the vice,
squeezed and grabbed the body,
looked into its little black eyes,
out came his Zippo,
flick,
a spark,
then hopping flames.

stopping dead in the road.
flattened, as a car put it out
with a merciful tyre
that didn't stop.

he's not around anymore.
enlisted the next year,
earliest he could,
looking to quench a thirst.
he went to Bosnia,
a desert, then a forest. a city, then back to the desert.
that's when he stopped moving.
scorched into the sand by a frog
bigger than him.

his thirst remained till the end.

for years, I still walked that lane.

crossed the path, tarmac, where the frog's shape
was,
like his...
forever burned — death's silhouette — scorched into the surface
beneath.
when it hopped
flaming
out of those shutters
in a last bid for freedom
despite the flames stealing what was left.

I wondered as I went on. for years later.
why
 I
was
left
marked by it more,
than frog, man or road.

stone cold lovers

lovers on a beach
wrapped in grains
claw-locked hands,
as sand flies hop
over matted hair
and seaweed strands.
sculpted bodies
stone-cold
with forgotten plans.

a lone parked car
rug still in the back
flask never opened,
food
to waste,
but for the birds
that can't get in.

they went together
to depart these lands.
dying birds and sinking ships
can't stop them,
now
together,
beached,
wrecked,
carcasses.
the dead make no plans.

[**First published with** *Close To The Bone 4.4.*, **November 2020**]

black and white to dead

we had a cat, back then, it was less than 5
like me
it wrapped itself about my head
it knew I shouldn't be hearing the sounds from the bedroom
next to mine
like she was in pain, tortured, worse.

she wasn't
a man was with her
making her, make those noises.

he once made similar noises
as he cut back the flesh on his foot,
released the ingrown nail
from his overgrown toe.
his tattoos came alive in the flicker of the fire
as he hacked away without any regard for his own flesh.
hairy and sweaty, he was.
and bloody.

he used to be in the army
fought then
was drunk now and with Mother
fighting still, maybe more than war.
a bruise there
cut here
my little portable tv out the window, there
gone.

he's gone now too...
to fight another battle.
she won't let him back in.
he lost that one.

we've a new tv
she lets me watch war films,
bloodier the better
in colour.
in them, I imagine him in bright crimsons
dying
over
and over, again.
a technicolour death.
the cat sits by me,
purring
it knows how these old ones always end.

down to the bone (on an 80s council estate)

Mother kicked me out
there were others; daily orphans of tired single parents
out into a cold frost, catching our breath on freezing eyelashes
hands sticking to the town's cast-iron lamposts

we were old enough to run
back then
and young enough to
run back,
when hurt,
like wounded animals, limping back to the fold

I was cut deep, to the bone
the knife we took had slipped through the stolen apple
I bled, dripped, turning ever-paler
I saw bone
turned green, like the apple, now streaked with my blood
I ran hard
dripping

she wouldn't let me in
I was kicked out for the day, maybe longer
whimpering like a dying limp
discarded
dog

she closed up, shut the door

the scar's still there
and now I'm old enough
that when I hurt,
like I do today,
more than I ever did then
I don't think
to go back
and it's when I should
and need it
most

not going back
to what was never there, to what I needed,
need now
I just bleed it out
alone
like back then
but, for the other poor bleeders with me
out there, with solace
knowing we're all
together;
more than alone

she had an itch

I travelled cities, proud,
telling them how she was;
beautiful, clever.
I showed photos
'Yes,' they'd say
and, 'how old?'

I told them,
and three times a day wasn't enough for her,
that I felt my age, plus ten
I couldn't stop talking about her.

the more I said,
the more I appealed to the crowd.
I left
didn't take a wiser offer.
knowing she was waiting,
for me.

I got back
the door was open
she'd fucked someone else,
he was still there, sunbathing out-back
whilst she was on the bed
waiting
wanting
more.

he'd only gone two rounds
I stayed,
for a while...
she really was something,
and nothing
I was tired from travelling.

haven't spoken since
didn't much
then.

[**First published with** *Close To The Bone 4.4.*, **November 2020**]

dead lucky

on my second smoke, hands-free, I looked into the night.
I breathed out; smoke rings, drifting to the moon.
my hands choke the life from him.
releasing a fraction, as he tried his last breath.
that was it;
all he was getting from me.

dry

'Get out, you're barred!'
the barman's voice went
unnoticed,
like the smashed mirror,
cowering punters,
spilt drinks
and emptying seats.

he pulled a gun, waved it about,
the barman ducked,
took cover,
we all did.

he threw it —
it didn't go off.

'Who's that?'
I said from beneath a table
'Dunno, I think he owns the place,'
a voice came
then he left.

the barman jumped up from behind cover,
locked the door.
as the last of the mirror fell to the counter
we finished our drinks
from a landlord
so drunk
he was barred from his own hole.

[First published with *Close To The Bone 4.4.*, **November 2020]**

ain't nobody home

ain't got put up with it
nobody does
home is just a word

girl, you go. before I do
you won't
put it to
me... no more...save a piece of me, whilst I still exist, we're
through

some said, through thick and thin — others, that the bottom has
dropped out
pain is waiting — it'll be less than whatever you call this, now

and, now

misery's a welcome warm pillow to me
an untouched scotch
no rocks needed
where I'll
B(e), B(e)... King.

how was it supposed to end?

it started through mist, smoke, strobes...
we couldn't see
(well enough to avoid each other)
we weren't really looking
lost in fumes of chaos
dancing off a misspent week

another drink
another go in for kiss
another head moves away

later,
2 am
it's all just wasters
the unmarried
the leftovers
scraps
and us,
the blind drunk
clearly visible, lights on
and alone

she said, take me home,
and so I did,
to hers
not that I knew where that was

in the earliest hours
after-sex minutes stretched to the sun
a new day and consequences strained to rise
when the drinks and ghosts rested
that house had a kids bedroom
where I looked for a toilet,
and another...when I was lost getting back to those legs

I'd been that kid
a broken toy
a single parent's collateral damage
after, I decided to hang around
until she realised I was just another one of them
a child in an adults body,
and
she had enough
arses to wipe.

too much, too little, too late

too big,
too fat,
too wide,
flat, brash or bold
bent over or tired
and old

too much of this,
of that
and
Hell, why not a change

life's
too short

off one bus
and onto another,
no time waiting around at a stop in the rain

it's...not you...it's me

a stone chiseled cliche,
I always had reasons
to go on,
hammering home their insecurities
walking past tears, into
my own smouldering heap
of regret

all dead fish
that never swam

an honest man would have looked hard
into himself
decided
he
was the one
floored,
not good enough
for them

by the time I learned this,
those past glories had become
my own ravines of hurt,
baggage,
scars and scabs
to face up to, then hide from
and
to keep hidden

by the time I had heart,
I was left looking over my shoulder
hoping those little marks didn't show through
bleed, run, seep,
and come to the surface
seen by that one in the end

that one I didn't think about way back then,
as I was cut, and was cutting
that one
I didn't think was deserved

but now exposed
as time burns short
I hope love is a blind faith

devoted,
I can't afford to run from this one
but wonder
if I did, unlike the rest,
would they be the one that follows?

so,
we can run towards the
noise together,
knowing the sun-bleached tides of life
are made sailable by all those
love-weathered mistakes.

a walk in the dunes

sweeping sands
carved, sculpted and shaped.
seasons captured in undulating mounds
rolling forever into the horizon.
mirroring the waves they confront.
sharp grassy peaks
and blown out bays,
hollows
and hideaways;
accenting changes, forever
in flux.

concrete boxes
are old war scars.
and incinerated wooded breaks;
sea blown victims.
a line of weed and carcasses;
rejects of the waters,
a line of dead between land and sea.

the body lay hidden
covered by a sandy shawl.
my shoes went in
and then legs, buckling.
the rancid air escaped
and days old sand,
sea and decay blew out
over the new.

past the crest
is a pitted hard plain
of heather.
hundreds of flowers
blues, bright whites and yellows
and trees taking root.
hanging on by
fragile tender tendrils.

as

over this crest
lives are re-beginning.
until the waters next overspill
and like the lost body in the sands,
she reclaims
what's her's.

[first published with *Necro Productions*]

I hurt, so you don't have to

there's a window in my head,
left open by hurt
it's where the rain gets in
the curtains were never closed
thick,
still,
they blot out the light
letting in dark.

on a clear day, I can see for miles
the curtains touch me
dank, damp and musty
memories of the darkness
shaping a perspective.

one day I'll fall out that window
land
in the flower beds
I'll look up to it, from below
and those dusty rank curtains
and,
I'll wonder how I ever made it
up there.

when I smell the roses
those thorns bursting my flesh
I'll remember...
I hurt,
so you didn't have to.

[**First published with** *Close To The Bone 4.4.*, **November 2020**]

respite for a slight return (forevermore)

engine stops
birds' voice.
wind moves trees.
at a distance, water moves small stones.
here
isolation is the gift,
and
contemplation brings questions...

go on?
back?
remain here...forevermore?

eyes close, dead weights pulled down,
to blacken out life.
the sounds become
everything.
they massage,
soothe.
a fragile soul is embraced,
trees and bird song join in harmony:
nature's caress.

go back?
stay here forevermore?

start engine,
attach pipe,
prepare to breathe the blackness,
the pain,
all down.
trees and birds.
peace in nature.
changes, ebbs, flows.
the engine is stopped.
I turn on the radio:
words,
interference,
white noise.

stay here forevermore?

a light starts through the trees.
one, two, three…then four
and then five
rays,
hope.
cut through
birds rejoice
and now those trees dance, in triumph.
a bandaged soul made strong in an age-old embrace.
the body returns,
mind defrosts,
eyes open.

I'll be
going on, not back.
forevermore
…for them.

happy little tales of melancholy madness

why'd you touch me,
if it felt like it burned?
how'd it feel — to do it anyway?
knowing that
and just
keep on
doing it...

or, was it a big
mistake?

I saw a boat.
I wanted,
desperately
to go,
to answer it.

so I thought

if it wasn't for the final mistake
if only I'd caught that damn fucking boat.
I'd be sainted, immortal.

one shot — all it took.

I would have been forever
carved
into trees,
a deep scratch,
initialled in stone,
two initials, alone.

now, it's blue Monday each day.
and every day's colours, painted black.
like the silhouettes the window's bars cast
on a cold concrete floor.

so you lived, bullet just passed through.
like me, I suppose.

and, before you go, to finish…just to say.
I miss you, but, I've never felt happier,

the burns from your touch, now
finally, fade.
as I tell these happy little tales of
melancholy madness
from my metaphoric prison of a bedsit
— I'm at peace.

one last note

she jumped off
from riding me like an angry jockey
she was scared, the blood on the sheets,
was it hers?
it was mine
not as delicate as
Beethoven,
she'd hammered at me like
Jerry-Lee,
ripped my piano string

time and place

I'd like to go back,
for a day,
maybe a night
not stay too long,
but long enough to remember;
that time
when I thought,
I had nothing,
but had it
all
that I was trapped and lonely,
but was free
and going nowhere,
to stay long enough to remember
not regret
and feel
the hangover
shame
with no one there to ease any of it.

like a scene from a bad book

she fell from the stage
like a drunken, polluted ballerina.
one leg stayed on,
the other reached three feet down for the floor
below the dance floor.
a spray of red went up the front of her
slip of a little white dress.

no one noticed, lost in a hedonistic haze.
no one but me.
they'd taken pills, to get lost,
I'd drank through, to be found.
I carried her out
no one was waiting.

to see through the smoke,
heads, sweat and the noise that vibrated the walls,
you had to look damn hard, to find another human being,
even though the place was full of bodies.

only sometimes, when you're really lost
you desire to be found, and to find.
I did, but it was too late,
for her
I'm left lost and found
underground
no way though
but maybe, to find the next dance floor, drink.
next time, to save one last soul before it's not too late.

fucking writers

stopped by a single word...

'You,' he said with his back to the intruder
was it a '?'
or '!'
after that word
I froze-up anyway.

he stopped me, in my tracks
caught my reflection in a picture
of a bluebird
as he typed up some world-tainted-shit
about drinking and fucking too much.

even if you had,
all of it,
was there ever,
too much?
then, he said it,
like he knew me,

'You.'

fucking writers.

pen mightier than the sword?
I had a .38
and he,
smacked me with a word
from his mouth
and the side of a 10-year-old MacBook.

'Goodnight Sweetheart,' he said.

'I'll finish it when I'm good and ready,
you'll get your pound of flesh,'

'fucking publishers,' he finished.

chasing Chinaski

love…is a mad dog
and
it's from Hell.
so he said
and he wrote.
something like that,
brutal words, like black ice
with heart.

I took the pen
sat at the desk
emptied the bottles
and chased him.
again
and again.
exhausted the verse,
stained the papers
with ink-like-blood.

words came out,
trying too hard
…or not hard enough.
word after word
came,
again
and again.
the same but not the same,
untrue.
without the heart.
his heart,
of stones and roses.

I left the desk
put down the pen.
gave in to love...and the mad dog from hell.
I moved outside
remembered my true pains;
protected by love.

I'd caught him up
but nothing was there of him,
there was:
me.

the words came back
with heart, in ink.
I picked up the pen
read them back
drank down the bottle.

he was always there,
right there beside me,
they all are.

dreams of future memories

broken windows cast fractured light,
cracked old boards, dust, mites.
an old wooden window
shares views to trees,
hills and sky;
ever-changing horizons,
now,
just for me.

in my chair, with
my bottle and a book,
making notes 'till dawn.
a rhythm, relentless flow,
a momentum.

nature rattles outside
aching to share
to revel
to get in and at me.
to touch those dreams and memories
that shake inside:
futures;
fictions made free...

as my mind escapes in fiction
my body is fixed back to our reality
like a lead weight
anchored to shore
one foot sits in her blood
as my mind's ink
chases her over horizons
we'll now never get to reach.

live brutalism (Idles band)

nervously pacing
back
and forth.
before on stage
going back
...and
then forth.

scratching at the dirt,
like a cockerel in heat.

raw nerves,
energy.
uncertain of receipt (modest).
so vehement in delivery.

he contemplates.

then, on stage,
there's fire.
in the crowds, even more,
the launch of an unstoppable force
of verve, beauty
...and control.

mechanical stoics
strike mental chords.

crowds shift,
perceptions break,
audiences grow.

reprogrammed

ideas will fly,
bar
to bar,
city
after city.

amongst the wreckage
free thoughts are sown.

peace, love, energy,
Idles (band).

blue rinsed pleasure boat

we kept it quiet 'till they got onboard
plugged in, but didn't let loose.
distortion pedal untouched
feedback and amps still to 3
not even 7.

It wept out of our eager limbs; lounge, jazz, some other 'life on hold'
beige frequencies to dull the senses.

they settled in
all those years between them —
the barge carried 2,400 years
and a hundred pugs' worth of wrinkles —
saggy skin touched the decks
hung over the sides and
the waters from the boat.

any requests?
Moon River?
we asked from the front.
hands poised,
plectrums glistened.

mischief.

a mutter from the back and we cranked it to 11.
QOTSA — Millionaire.
Next up... Metallica.

that first real note got them moving
scrambling
adjusting the hearing aids
launching themselves overboard,
swimming for their lives,
or, a merciful passing propeller to end the noise.
swimming to shore,
away.

but for two,
they
stayed.
they weren't done with living yet.
bleeding ears, and blue rinses
didn't matter now.
they wanted to get to the solo
and by then
even our ears tired and fingers would bleed.
these old bastards wouldn't budge.
a life's punishment behind those cataracts
and they stood still
as if our future selves.

a drink with the battered old-timers
we'd pick their friends up, out of the water, on the way down-stream.
they could tell us about their own songs
see if we want to jump ship,
before we too aged,
and gave up listening,
before the good bit;
life's solo.

the Duke

the Duke walks on water
downing a triple rum n' coke.
he falls from tables,
dancing, with a tip of his hat.
he falls...
into the arms of many girls.
they wait
oh so eager to catch.
he doesn't spill a drop.

he plays the field
and the field plays him.
it's not a real-game.
he flirts with many,
toys with the chosen few,
taking home just one or two.

the Duke abides by his own rules
in politics, music and science.
the Duke has no time for dogma;
sees through the lies and facts.
the Duke eyes another place
of realities between the layers;
time, space and
our place in the stars.

the Duke faced Death — Death ran away.

the Duke plays guitar,
better than the bands he sees.

the Duke goes on, unstoppable,
leaving me in the dust,
free-willed, free-thinking, freestyling.

long live the Duke.

[**First published with** *Bristol Noir*]

a red dress

a hangover from school to college,
the lies they told,
the lack of confidence and self-depreciation leading him to believe
them,
then
and now.
'Man, you not popped your cherry yet? I lost mine when I was born.'
(this guy really hadn't thought it through — sick mother fucker).
still, he berated on him.

relentless

he said, take the fifty,
take a walk.
in the car park — he pointed
there's a girl,
she'll take a fuck, make you a real man.
he took the notes.
he handed it away, clean, guilt-free;
took nothing from her.

(and she gave him respect)

more of a man than they'd ever be...
so it began:
journey into real (man).

whatever that is.

[**First published with** *Bristol Noir*]

hell-tail bitch

she sells it,
and not for money.
with each arch of that back,
kick of that tail
she milks
crushes
gnaws
grinds lose,
another piece of man-soul.

the dogs, they queue up for it,
to give it to her,
knowing they're not first in line,
that
they're
mixing each and everyone's
soup.
and go in anyway,
deeper.

she'll always sell
and they'll all want it,
everyone,
men,
even some of the women too.

God can't resist,
he'll take her at last
and she'll walk away
riding to eternity,
feeling nothing,
taking everything.

[First published with *Close To The Bone 4.4.*, November 2020]

what crows know about death

they dig at the dirt, scratching up worms
fly past, ignoring each other — except to compete
for those worms.

but, when one of them drops,
the hourglass freezes.
and as its blood stills
feathers and wings rest.

they look on,
they know death
that it's coming.

then — it's back to the worms,
busy, digging, scratching, toiling away
day after tiring day.
after all,
what else is there?
in the end,
we're all just food
for those worms.

the crows know.
try,
to get them first.
but also know,
it won't stop what's coming.

people are complex

there's one:
sounds like an architect,
looks like a cage fighter.

another:
plasters that ceiling, like a pro, an artist.
as he sways back and forth,
the beer cans below him filling up the bucket.

one more:
manages to keep the place afloat.
maids are happy, waiters paid.
except the government.
the taxman can wait.

and another:
wears the uniform with pride,
part of a brotherhood.
doesn't shoot back.
he'll take a bullet himself first.

and a mother:
food on the table,
mouths fed,
watered.
but for her own.

me?

I'll pull your heart right out
in front of you,
feel its last beat,
as I distract you with these words.

wash it off, stay inside, don't go abroad and stay home

we looked for UFOs, ghosts through the trees.
lights from passing cars on the road behind lit up our imaginations
in the evergreens.
made the branches dance,
where there was
prancing spectres, ghouls
and angels.
demons too,
spinning out of those tree limbs.

get inside now, they shouted, RUN!
something real had broken our fantasies.
an incident,
an explosion,
a broken thing in a factory far away
in a country we hadn't heard of
might as well be Mars,
aliens in a foreign land.

the rain brought it down,
radiation, they said.
a shower later, and the foreign land was far away, again,
and the ghosts danced, again,
the trees swayed.

then it came.
tales of lambs born,
with legs on their backs,
three-eyed babies,
glowing piss...flowing.
all this stopped the ghosts playing.
for a mistake in a foreign land,
trapped us inside, trying to shower,
over and over again.
but, it wouldn't ever come off.

great gig in the sky

a car abandoned near the bridge.
key in the ignition,
small cash withdrawn,
passport missing.

he should have gone home,
whilst he still had one.
home is where there's heart.
he was loved all over —
for real.

we once saw a tattoo, in Singapore,
an arm around a Thai girl,
and wondered,
could it be...?
a hidden hero
a haunted poet, in a disgrace
of his own making.

and we hoped not...
that, instead, he's on an island,
with Elvis,
Kurt,
Amy,
Jimi
and Buddy.
singing and playing to lucky sunsets and sundowns
over serene sands.

I'm sold.

pack my bags,
sell me a ticket,
I'm catching that boat
to the best fucking gig ever.

dead birds and sinking ships

we all once flew,
floated
above the tides
and stayed up there
above the skies
rode the oceans

just about.

a drink, girl
soul(s) crushed,
rung dry
a job at a time...

now, we mourn all of us — fucked
we're nothing, but,
dead birds and sinking ships.

last words and all the places happy is

reams of empty canvases,
untouched lumps of uncarved wood.
empty lines, pens untouched,

years unlived.

kisses not tasted,
hands not held.
eyes dry. no tears,
of joy, or laughter.

sheets of empty beds,
lights that twinkle on dying trees with presents
unopened.
glasses full,
meals not tasted.
stories never told.

is anyone ever really happy?
what's the point? she said.
then left us.

for all this, you'll be missed.
for that is the space your happiness would have filled.
all the places you should have been,
before that little cell grew,
took you, too soon.
before the story was told.
you didn't even get to
read my first line.

and that would have made you happy, too.

bat versus cat

he's a real hard stoic, Batman
so, is Fred though...the cat

Batman stands hard against the rain,
the bullets, swinging fists, family loss,
the relentless torment of dementors attacking the moral fabric
of his city.

Fred licks the space where his balls once were,
looking to the moon, knowing
the door will be opened,
the food will be waiting.
thinking,
they'll always be another bird to eye up,
to jump.
just not the sort his missing balls were for.

Fred knows
life and love is a long haul endurance,
a trial.

as he calmly sits
under the bench, as freezing rain crashes over the sides
he believes the door will eventually open, the bowl will be out
as it always has been.
and when he stops believing this.
it'll be the end.

Printed in Great Britain
by Amazon